THE OFFICIAL
CHELSEA FC
ANNUAL 2011

Written by Rick Glanvill

A Grange Publication

© 2010. Published by Grange Communications Ltd., Edinburgh under licence from Chelsea FC Merchandising Limited. www.chelseafc.com. Printed in the EU.

Photographs © Press Association Images and Getty Images

ISBN: 978-1-907104-62-6

£7.99

INTRODUCTION 2011

What a great Chelsea annual this one was to do! Thanks to Carlo and the boys, 2009/10 was the most successful season in the club's entire history, so there were a lot of good things to write about – and it's always nice to look back on so much success.

Hope you enjoy all the pics, facts and features. And here's to more of the same in 2010/11!

CONTENTS

Chelsea FC : The Honours List

During the 2009/10 season the Blues added three more trophies to the trophy cabinet at Stamford Bridge: the Premier League, the FA Cup and the Community Shield. Here is an updated list of what the club has won since 1905.

FIRST TEAM

» **LEAGUE TITLE** *(four times)*
2009/10, 2005/6, 2004/5 *(Premier League)*
1954/5 *(Football League)*

» **FA CUP** *(six times)*
2010, 2009, 2007, 2000, 1997, 1970

» **UEFA CUP-WINNERS' CUP** *(twice)*
1998, 1971

» **UEFA SUPER CUP** *(once)*
1998

» **LEAGUE CUP** *(four times)*
2006/7, 2004/5, 1997/8, 1964/5

» **COMMUNITY SHIELD** *(four times)*
2009, 2005, 2000, 1955

YOUTH TEAM

» **FA YOUTH CUP** *(three times)*
2009/10, 1960/1, 1959/60

» **DIVISION TWO CHAMPIONS** *(twice)*
1989, 1984

» **FULL MEMBERS' CUP** *(twice)*
1990, 1986

CHAMPIONS!

No English team has ever won the title in the way Chelsea did on the last day of the season – by demolishing Wigan 8-0! As incredible as that scoreline was, it was much more important just to win, and the Blues finished one point ahead of arch rivals Man United to win the league for the fourth time in our history. The celebrations were as brilliant as in 2005 – if not even better.

The whole squad celebrates a famous win.

Look how much it meant to JT, Lamps and Ash when the final whistle went and the title was ours again.

One group of supporters had prepared their own t-shirt celebration in the stands.

Didier was desperate to win the Golden Boot, and grabbed himself a hat-trick of goals.

Carlo and Malouda raced down the line in front of supporters with the trophy.

And Ash made it 8-0 with a wicked shot…

Let's not forget the manager and all his backroom staff who played their part in the triumph.

Ashley Cole opened his account at home to bitter rivals Spurs and set the Blues up for a 3-0 rout. He scored four in an injury-hit season.

New signing Yury Zhirkov returned from injury in the Blues' home win over Porto on the opening night of the Champions League. Nicolas Anelka scored the winner – he scored four of the goals in our seven 1-0 wins.

Sun 9 Aug - Man Utd (Wembley) Community Shield D 2-2; Carvalho 52, Lampard 71. Att: 85,896 (Chelsea won 4-1 on penalties)

Sat 15 Aug - Hull City H PL W 2-1; Drogba 37, 90. Att: 41,597

Tue 18 Aug - Sunderland A PL W 3-1; Ballack 52, Lampard 61p, Deco 70. Att: 41,179

Sun 23 Aug - Fulham A PL W 2-0; Drogba 39, Anelka 76. Att: 25,404

Sat 29 Aug - Burnley H PL W 3-0; Anelka 45, Ballack 47, Cole, A 52. Att: 40,906

Sat 12 Sep - Stoke City A PL W 2-1; Drogba 45, Malouda 90. Att: 27,440

Tue 15 Sep - FC Porto H CL W 1-0; Anelka 48. Att: 39,436

Key: PL - Premier League, CL – Champions League, FAC – FA Cup, LC – League Cup, aet – after extra time, og – own goal.

8

How the Double was won...

Winning our first ever League and FA Cup Double was never easy, but there were plenty of amazing moments to savour. Enjoy them all over again with our season review.

Carlo Ancelotti's first game in charge of Chelsea was the Community Shield at Wembley, and it ended in a 2-2 draw. The Italian won his first silverware when Giggs and Evra failed from the spot in the penalty shootout, while Frank Lampard, Michael Ballack, Didier Drogba and Salomon Kalou all scored theirs.

The biggest crowd of the season at Stamford Bridge in early October saw Nicolas Anelka score on the hour against title hopefuls Liverpool. Florent Malouda (pictured) netted a second late on. First blood to the Blues!

Against Atlético Madrid in the Champions League, Salomon Kalou scored his side's first two goals in an impressive 4-0 victory over the Spanish outfit.

Sun 20 Sep - Tottenham H PL W 3-0; Cole, A 32, Ballack 58, Drogba 63. Att: 41,623

Wed 23 Sep - QPR H LC W 1-0; Kalou 52. Att: 37,781

Sat 26 Sep - Wigan A PL L 1-3; Drogba 47. Att: 18,542

Wed 30 Sep - APOEL Nicosia A CL W 1-0; Anelka 18. Att: 20,000

Sun 04 Oct - Liverpool H PL W 2-0; Anelka 60, Malouda 90. Att: 41,732

Sat 17 Oct - A Villa A PL L 1-2; Drogba 15. Att: 39,047

Wed 21 Oct - Atlético Madrid H CL W 4-0; Kalou 41, 52, Lampard 69, Perea 90og. Att: 39,997

2nd LEAGUE POSITION

The first league meeting between title favourites Chelsea and United in early November ended in a critical 1-0 win for the Blues. John Terry glanced the winner in from Frank Lampard's free kick. Carlo's men were now five points clear.

In late November Chelsea set up progress into the knockout stages of the Champions League with a crucial win at the Stadio do Dragao, home of Porto. Nicolas Anelka brilliantly headed the only goal from Florent Malouda's pinpoint cross.

The Blues' 3-0 win at the Emirates was one of the team performances of the season. 'Men against boys', the media agreed afterwards, and didn't JT enjoy it!

Sat 24 Oct - Blackburn H PL W 5-0; Givet 20og, Lampard 48, 59p, Essien 52, Drogba 64. Att: 40,836

Wed 28 Oct - Bolton H LC W 4-0; Kalou 15, Malouda 26, Deco 67, Drogba 89. Att: 41,538

Sat 31 Oct - Bolton A PL W 4-0; Lampard 45p, Deco 61, Ivanovic 82, Drogba 90. Att: 22,680

Tue 03 Nov - Atlético Madrid A CL D 2-2; Drogba 82, 88. Att: 45,000

Sun 08 Nov - Man Utd H PL W 1-0; Terry 76. Att: 41,836

Sat 21 Nov - Wolves H PL W 4-0; Malouda 5, Essien 12, 22, Cole, J 56. Att: 41,786

Wed 25 Nov - Porto A CL W 1-0; Anelka 69. Att: 35,000

Sun 29 Nov - Arsenal A PL W 3-0; Drogba 41, 86, Vermaelen 45og. Att: 60,067

Wed 2 Dec - Blackburn A LC D 3-3 aet; Drogba 48, Kalou 52, Ferreira 120. Att: 18,136 (Blackburn won on penalties)

Key: PL - Premier League, CL – Champions League, FAC – FA Cup, LC – League Cup, aet – after extra time, og – own goal.

How the Double was won...

"After 15 games the opponent was able to cover the space between the lines in our team so we changed. After the first half against Fulham at Christmas when we were losing, we changed to use two wingers to open the pitch and use all the space to attack"

– Carlo Ancelotti

Salomon Kalou celebrated the own goal that meant Chelsea beat Fulham 2-1 at Christmas. The three home points were priceless and looked unlikely until Chris Smalling turned into his own net.

The FA Cup campaign started with a bang in January when Danny Sturridge scored his first goal since arriving from Man City. Watford were eventually dispatched 5-0 and the Blues' defence of the trophy was up and running.

Sat 5 Dec - Man City A PL L 1-2; Adebayor 8og. Att: 47,348

Tue 8 Dec - APOEL Nicosia H CL D 2-2; Essien 19, Drogba 26. Att: 40,917

Sat 12 Dec - Everton H PL D 3-3; Drogba 18, 59, Anelka 23. Att: 41,579

Wed 16 Dec - Portsmouth H PL W 2-1; Anelka 23, Lampard 79p. Att: 40,137

Sun 20 Dec - West Ham A PL D 1-1; Lampard 61p. Att: 33,388

Sat 26 Dec - Birmingham A PL D 0-0. Att: 28,958

Mon 28 Dec - Fulham H PL W 2-1; Drogba 73, Smalling 75og. Att: 41,805

Sun 3 Jan - Watford H FAC W 5-0; Sturridge 5, 68, Eustace 15og, Malouda 22, Lampard 64. Att: 40,912

1st LEAGUE POSITION

Chelsea scored seven or more in four league games at the Bridge, and the first was Sunderland in mid-January. It was the club's first 7-up since 1960, and meant a busy day for their poor goalie Martin Fulop.

Arsenal were supposed to be back in the title race before they came to Fulham Road but they left in tatters once Didier Drogba had torn them apart. The on-fire striker scored both goals, including the scorcher pictured here.

Sat 16 Jan - Sunderland H PL W 7-2; Anelka 8, 65, Malouda 17, Cole, A 22, Lampard 34, 90, Ballack 52. Att: 41,776

Sat 23 Jan - Preston N.E. A FAC W 2-0, Anelka 37, Sturridge 47. Att: 23,119

Wed 27 Jan - Birmingham H PL W 3-0; Malouda 5, Lampard 32, 90. 41,293

Sat 30 Jan - Burnley A PL W 2-1; Anelka 27, Terry 82. Att: 21,131

Tue 2 Feb - Hull City A PL D 1-1; Drogba 42. Att: 24,957

Sun 7 Feb - Arsenal H PL W 2-0; Drogba 8, 23. Att: 41,794

Wed 10 Feb - Everton A PL L 1-2; Malouda 17. Att: 36,411

Key: PL - Premier League, CL – Champions League, FAC – FA Cup, LC – League Cup, aet – after extra time, og – own goal.

How the Double was won...

"We conceded some goals but also scored a lot from set-pieces, and won important games, [such as] the last game against Arsenal"

– Carlo Ancelotti

Another Drog-inspired win at Wolves – he scored both goals in the 2-0 victory and set us back on the title track.

Progress towards the FA Cup final continued, but Chelsea's hopes of winning the Champions League were extinguished by an old flame – José Mourinho. Chelsea had goalies Cech and Hilario out injured, Inter won 3-1 over two legs and the lowest point in Chelsea's season was reached.

The Blues failed to build on beating Arsenal and surprisingly lost at Everton days later, despite taking the lead. The Toffees were sticky opponents and won 2-1.

Sat 13 Feb - Cardiff City H FAC W 4-1; Drogba 2, Ballack 51, Sturridge 69, Kalou 86. Att: 40,827

Sat 20 Feb - Wolves A PL W 2-0; Drogba 40, 67. Att: 28,978

Wed 24 Feb - Internazionale A CL L 1-2; Kalou 51. Att: 84,638

Sat 27 Feb - Man City H PL L 2-4; Lampard 42, 90p. Att: 41,814

Sun 7 Mar - Stoke City H FAC W 2-0; Lampard 35, Terry 67. Att: 41,322

Sat 13 Mar - West Ham H PL W 4-1; Alex 16, Drogba 56, 90, Malouda 77. Att: 41,755

Tue 16 Mar - Internazionale H CL L 0-1. Att: 38,107

1st LEAGUE POSITION

It was possibly the strangest atmosphere at Anfield ever as many home supporters preferred Chelsea winning the title to Man Utd. Frank Lampard scored the second goal, and knew exactly how important it was.

Didier Drogba started on the bench and Wayne Rooney missed out, but Chelsea virtually wrenched the title out of United's grip with a fantastic 2-1 win at Old Trafford in early April. Joe Cole (pictured) netted the first by back-flicking a pass from the outstanding Florent Malouda.

Sun 21 Mar - Blackburn A PL D 1-1; Drogba 6. Att: 25,554

Wed 24 Mar - Portsmouth A PL W 5-0; Drogba 32, 77, Malouda 50, 60, Lampard 90. Att: 18,753

Sat 27 Mar - A Villa H PL W 7-1; Lampard 15, 44p, 62p, 90, Malouda 57, 68, Kalou 83. Att: 41,825

Sat 3 Apr - Man Utd A PL W 2-1; Cole, J 20, Drogba 79. Att: 75,217

Sat 10 Apr - A Villa (Wembley) FAC W 3-0; Drogba 67, Malouda 89, Lampard 90. Att: 85,472

Tue 13 Apr - Bolton H PL W 1-0; Anelka 43. Att: 40,539

Sat 17 Apr - Tottenham A PL L 1-2; Lampard 90. Att: 35,814

Key: PL - Premier League, CL – Champions League, FAC – FA Cup, LC – League Cup, aet – after extra time, og – own goal.

How the Double was won...

"That's what it's all about – winning – and we want that feeling again and again"
— *John Terry*

Winning 5-0 in the disaster zone of Portsmouth was one thing, but demolishing Aston Villa was something very special. The morale-boosting 7-1 saw Frank Lampard pass the 150-goal mark too.

With Ashley Cole out injured for two months left-back Yury Zhirkov made his mark, especially in the FA Cup semi-final at Wembley. His attacking down the left was vital to the Blues' 3-0 win.

A confidence-boosting win was just what was needed before the decisive league trip to Liverpool and Stoke were the 7-0 victims of Chelsea's now unstoppable surge towards the league championship. Florent Malouda, the star of the run-in, scored the Blues' seventh.

In a season that he won the Golden Boot it had to be Didier Drogba who scored the winner in the FA Cup final against Portsmouth. The well-earned win made it three FA Cup winners' medals for the Ivorian star, who now has six goals in six Wembley finals.

Sun 25 Apr - Stoke City H PL W 7-0;
Kalou 24, 31, 68, Lampard 44p, 81, Sturridge 87, Malouda 89. Att: 41,013
Sun 2 May - Liverpool A PL W 2-0; Drogba 33, Lampard 54. Att: 44,375
Sun 9 May - Wigan H PL W 8-0;
Anelka 6, 56, Lampard 32p, Kalou 54, Drogba 63, 68p, 80, Cole, A 90. Att: 41,383
Sat 15 May - Portsmouth (Wembley) FAC W 1-0; Drogba 59. Att: 88,335

1st LEAGUE POSITION

Tour the home of the Champions!

Go behind-the-scenes at the world-famous Stamford Bridge, home to Chelsea Football Club and have your photo taken with the Barclays Premier League trophy and FA Cup.

To book call **0871 984 1955** *or email **tours@chelseafc.com**
www.chelseafc.com/tours

Lines open Monday to Friday 9am – 5pm. Tours do not run on home matchdays or the day before home Champions League games.
All tours are subject to availability, cancellation and alteration at late notice. Trophy photos subject to availability and additional charge.

CHELSEA FIRST TEAM PLAYERS

TO HAVE ANY CHANCE AGAINST OUR BRILLIANT GOALIES...

1 PETR CECH

40 HENRIQUE HILARIO

22 ROSS TURNBULL

THEY FIRST HAVE TO GET PAST OUR AMAZING DEFENDERS...

2 BRANISLAV IVANOVIC

3 ASHLEY COLE

26 JOHN TERRY

17 JOSE BOSINGWA

18 YURY ZHIRKOV

33 ALEX

7 RAMIRES

19 PAULO FERREIRA

43 JEFFREY BRUMA

5 MICHAEL ESSIEN

10 YOSSI BENAYOUN

8 FRANK LAMPARD

12 MIKEL

15 FLORENT MALOUDA

44 GAEL KAKUTA

SAM HUTCHINSON

With special thanks to Sam Hutchinson who has retired from play but will continue to work with the club.

THANKS AND FAREWELL TO ...

DECO

RICARDO CARVALHO

BUT THEY WILL STILL NEVER STOP OUR ATTACKERS...

21 SALOMON KALOU

11 DIDIER DROGBA

23 DANIEL STURRIDGE

45 FABIO BORINI

39 NICOLAS ANELKA

JOE COLE

MICHAEL BALLACK

JULIANO BELLETTI

MIROSLAV STOCH

What it means to be DOUBLE WINNERS...

Has it sunk in yet? Are you still excited about winning the League, the FA Cup, not to mention the Community Shield? The statistics show Chelsea are only the seventh English club to win the 'Double'. The prize money for winning may help buy new players, and the glory might convince others to join the best club in the world.

But what else does winning the Double bring to the players, manager and supporters? Here are a few we like:

Wear gold badges

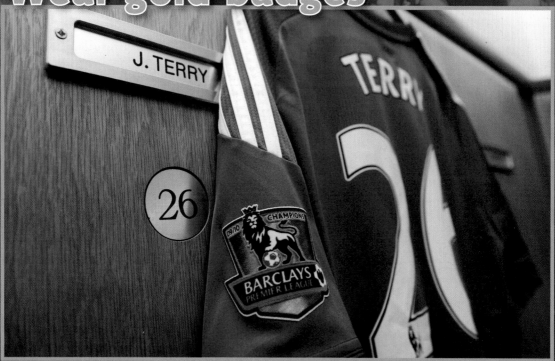

In the whole of the Premier League teams, only Chelsea's players will be able to wear special gold Premier League badges as reigning champions. And of course loyal Blues are the only supporters who can wear gold badges on the sleeves of replica shirts. This is a picture of John Terry's new shirt, ready and waiting for the great man to put it on for season 2010/11.

Can you see: the special gold Premier League badge? John Terry's name plate, and his number on his changing room locker? Is it the same as his shirt number?

And a few more to listen out for...

TV and radio commentators will keep calling Chelsea 'the champions' or 'the FA Cup holders'. Which always sounds nice!

Chelsea fans can sing 'Champions! Champions!' or (before kick-off) 'Bring on the champions!' from August right through to May. Sweet!

And finally, it means every single one of us Chelsea supporters is a Double champion!

Carlo Ancelotti won more in his first season at Stamford Bridge than any other Chelsea manager.

Getting personal with trophies

After the FA Cup final, Chelsea manager Carlo Ancelotti and chairman Bruce Buck posed for cameras next to all of the trophies won. The FA Cup and Premier League Trophy will actually be in the Chelsea museum at Stamford Bridge for the whole season. That means only Blues fans can see the two pieces of silverware and have their photograph taken with them at our home ground.

Just imagine, if jealous United or Arsenal fans want to see the trophies, they have to catch the tube to Fulham Broadway!

Defend the titles

Carlo Ancelotti won more in his first season at Stamford Bridge than any other Chelsea manager. He also made history by winning the Blues the Double for the first time.

Last season's success means that as Man United are defending just the League Cup trophy, and Liverpool, Arsenal, Manchester City, Tottenham and everyone else won nothing, Carlo Ancelotti went into the 2010/11 season with three times as many titles to hold onto as the rest.

TOP DROG :
Didier's Golden Goals

Didier Drogba was awarded the Golden Boot for being the Premier League's top marksman in season 2009/10. Don't forget he was away for a month at the Africa Cup of Nations as well! Here are six of the best among his 29 goals in 32 appearances.

Direct – Hull City home Drog scored the first league goals of Carlo's reign at the Bridge on the opening day. His first was a wonderful free kick effortlessly steered past the Tigers 'keeper Myhill. 1-0.

29 goals in
32 appearances

Stealthy - Liverpool away Brilliantly latching on to Gerrard's soft back-pass, Didier rounded goalie Reina and hit the back of the net to set-up a crucial victory at Anfield. 1-0.

Priceless – Man Utd away Good work and a clever pass from Salomon opened up United's defence, and substitute Didier delivered once again with a powerful blast past Van der Sar. 2-0.

Ruthless – Arsenal home Arsenal attack is broken up. Frank finds Didier down the right. Didier leaves Clichy and Vermaelen in his wake. Didier whacks the ball past Manuel Almunia. 2-0.

Boot-ylicious – Wigan home Our Ivorian legend clinched the Golden Boot with a hat-trick in the 8-0 slaughter of Wigan. None was better than this powerful close-range header. 5-0.

Classy – Bolton away Nico chips, Deco chests, Frank flicks and Didier steers the ball past Jaaskelainen. A goal of sheer quality. 4-0.

Spot the Ball

Study the pictures below closely, then use your skill
to spot where you think the balls might be.

A

B

Answers on page 61.

Chelsea History Lesson:

CHELSEA

FOOTBALL CLUB
v
REAL MADRID
European Cup-Winners' Cup Final
At the KARAISKAKI STADIUM, ATHENS
Wednesday, 19th May, 1971 (KICK-OFF 7.30 p.m.)
OFFICIAL PROGRAMME 10p (2/-)

Even though the match was played in Greece, Chelsea produced a match programme in English and sold it in Athens.

DID YOU KNOW?
Chelsea won a European trophy two years before Liverpool did!

1971
CUP KINGS OF EUROPE

We would all love to see Chelsea win the Champions League at Wembley in May, but 2011 is also the 40th anniversary of the year the Blues famously won our first European trophy: the Uefa Cup-Winners' Cup. Look who we beat in the final...

In the quarter-final Chelsea came back from a 0-2 defeat in Belgium to beat Bruges 4-2. Peter 'Ossie' Osgood returned from injury to score twice at the Bridge.

Chelsea played fellow English team Manchester City over two legs in the semi-final. The first game at Stamford Bridge was young South African forward Derek Smethurst's greatest moment. He scored the only goal of the game. City's goalie knocked the ball into his own net at Maine Road, so Chelsea triumphed 2-0 on aggregate.

Dave Sexton and his team faced the famous Real Madrid in the final, which was played in Athens on 19 May 1971. The 'King of Stamford Bridge,' Peter Osgood, scored for the Blues, but the game ended in a 1-1 draw. A replay took place in the same city two days later. Defender John Dempsey opened the scoring but this time Ossie added a second (pictured). The Spanish legends pulled one back, but Chelsea won 2-1 to claim the Uefa Cup-Winners' Cup for the first time.

The players enjoyed the usual open-top bus ride among hundreds of thousands of Blues supporters around Fulham. Kings of Europe!

It was smiles and high-fives all round in May when superstar Didier joined in a match at Cobham to launch Help a London Child's new project 'Sport in the City'. Imagine tackling the Drog!

GIVING SOMETHING BACK

Hitting the net is not the only type of goal that Chelsea Football Club goes for each season. The club also aims to give a lot back to the community, especially local youngsters.

We've been busy supporting our chosen charity, Help a London Child, but we've had lots of fun along the way too!

Chelsea tries to help young footballers with an Asian background aged 8-13 break into football with the Asian Star project. Hundreds of boys travel from all over the country to test their skills at Cobham and earn a place at Chelsea's summer trials. Several winners have already joined academies at professional football clubs.

HELP A LONDON CHILD

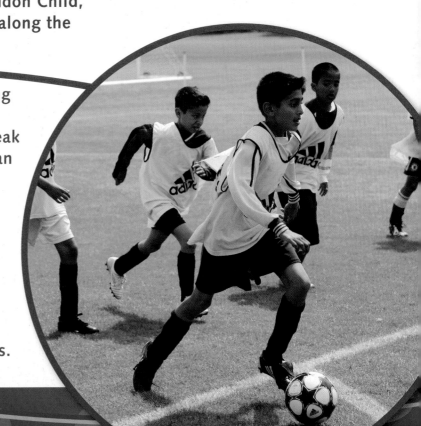

MARATHON LION!

Chelsea's very own Stamford the Lion ran the London Marathon on the day the Blues beat Stoke 7-0. He raised more than £11,000 in sponsorship for 'Help a London Child,' and here's how he did it...

Our determined mascot reached the finishing 26-mile line – without stopping to chase any zebras on the way – and came out in front of the crowd at Stamford Bridge to a big round of applause.

GIVING SOMETHING BACK
RIGHT TO PLAY

Since confirming Right To Play as our global charity partner in 2005, Chelsea have been heavily involved in raising vital funds for many of the charity's initiatives. Right To Play is an athlete-driven international humanitarian organisation that uses sport and play programmes to improve health, develop life skills and foster peace for children and communities in some of the most disadvantaged areas of the world affected by war, poverty and disease.

For example, in July 2009, the entire Chelsea team took part in a massive fundraising event displaying their skills and coaching children at the Right To Play Sports Day. Stars from the worlds of rugby, tennis, swimming and even free running were all on hand to coach children in their sport throughout the day. Five-time Olympic gold medalist and Chelsea fan Sir Steve Redgrave and former England rugby captain Will Carling were just two of the many sports celebrities involved. The event raised hundreds of thousands of pounds and is one of the biggest any club has been involved in.

First team coach Ray Wilkins said afterwards 'It has been an incredible event. I thought it was going to be big but it is far bigger than I anticipated. Also, it has not only been supported by us but by so many other sports people as well. And it's all brilliant for the charity, the fund raising is the most important thing and as far as that is concerned this event has done a fantastic job.'

Early in 2010, Chelsea donated £50,000 to Right To Play's programmes in Uganda, impacting on the lives of thousands of children who face poverty, war and disease every day. These children have now been given access to programmes that will dramatically enhance their health and well-being thanks to funding from the club.

Chelsea has also supported the United against Malaria initiative – a campaign to change people's behaviour by encouraging families to sleep under nets and take other steps to beat the disease by the next World Cup in 2014. The club teamed up with Right To Play to help distribute 3,000 mosquito nets along with cards with educational messages from Michael Essien and Didier Drogba and other African sporting legends.

Chelsea's Right To Play ambassador, Michael Essien, said 'We are very excited to play a role in this campaign. It's fantastic that Right To Play have been given these nets to distribute – it will help save so many lives. We recognize that if we are to virtually end malaria deaths it requires a huge effort from every individual. It is exciting to see how through sport and in particular football, we can help bring awareness to this campaign.'

CHELSEA AT THE SOUTH AFRICA 2010 FIFA WORLD CUP

The Chelsea squad had 12 players from five different teams in South Africa last summer. It would have been more, but Mikel (Nigeria), Michael Ballack (Germany) and Michael Essien (Ghana) were all injured and could not play any part. It was not the best tournament for Chelsea's players, but here's how they each fared.

ENGLAND
(reached last 16, lost to Germany)

ASHLEY COLE
Even though England had a disappointing World Cup, Ash performed well.

JOHN TERRY
This dive to block a shot against Slovenia showed how much playing for his country means to JT. A leader on the pitch. As always.

JOE COLE
His last England tournament as a Blue. Hardly used by Fabio Capello and could do little when on as a sub in the Germany defeat.

FRANK LAMPARD
Frank will always be remembered for his 'goal' that was not given against Germany. His brilliant shot bounced well over the line and would have made the score 2-2.

FRANCE
(out in group stage)

FLORENT MALOUDA
Flo was not used enough by his manager, but scored France's only goal in a 1-2 defeat against hosts South Africa.

NICOLAS ANELKA
A very short trip for Nico, who was sent home after an argument with France manager Raymond Domenech. France players went on strike to support the Chelsea striker.

CHELSEA AT THE SOUTH AFRICA 2010 FIFA WORLD CUP

PORTUGAL
(reached last 16, lost to Spain)

PAULO FERREIRA
Started well against Ivory Coast, but lost out to Valencia right-back Ricardo Costa after that.

DECO
Dogged by injury, the Brazilian-born midfielder was only able to play in one match, the 0-0 draw with Drogba and Kalou's Ivory Coast.

RICARDO CARVALHO
The ever-present rock of a very defensive Portugal side. Just what he needed after an injury-hit season with Chelsea.

IVORY COAST
(out in the group stage)

DIDIER DROGBA
Broke his arm in a warm-up match and never looked fully fit despite brave performances in a very tough group. Scored his only goal against the mighty Brazil.

SALOMON KALOU
Started two games and scored in one. Carried on the confidence he showed for Chelsea in the title run-in, and always made things happen for the 'Elephants.'

SERBIA
(out in the group stage)

BRANISLAV IVANOVIC
Chelsea's popular defender played well in all three matches but was let down by his attacking teammates' finishing against Australia. The Aussies beat Serbia 2-1 to send both teams out.

Spot the
Difference

Study the two pictures below closely, then try to
spot the 6 differences between them.

Answers page 61.

WORDSEARCH

The surnames of 20 Chelsea managers are mixed up in the grid below. They go up, down, backwards or diagonally. Can you spot them all? Which one was the first to win a trophy in 1955?

```
R D C F G M P M G D W I L K I N S C
K D L A S H E L L I T O J K R D A Y
R R L C L M C C R E A D I E L M H T
L F N S Z D N H X V T N W E P B L R
N N H C Z R E B K K G O I B T I C E
P O C O N T Z R L Z L F E T T M V H
M T N L L V B R H F R L N T Q I F C
W H R A X L H O H E L Q O W N L H O
L G D R F Y H C T T A L W W Q L I D
M I R I N N N R D F E D Z R K A D N
F N T M I A O C B C K M L H R I D L
M K T R L P R E N T N B T L M V I M
X L U B K H C A K N I T I D T C N D
M O B M O N R N N A W L X R H V K N
M Y K D W L M Q Y H R T L R R M M K
Z L D N C N O T X E S D F U X E L F
Z L R P Z H N N Y X Q R T B G M L N
E W M P R Y L Y I R E I N A R R R L
```

Ancelotti	Knighton
Birrell	Mccreadie
Blanchflower	Mourinho
Calderhead	Porterfield
Campbell	Ranieri
Docherty	Scolari
Drake	Sexton
Gullit	Shellito
Hiddink	Vialli
Hoddle	Wilkins

Answers page 61.

YOUTH CUP GLORY AGAIN – AFTER 49 YEARS!

Dermot Drummy's Chelsea Academy Under-18s won the coveted FA Youth Cup trophy for the first time since 1961, beating Aston Villa 3-2 over two legs.

It was just reward for a brilliant campaign that the team bossed from start to finish. It's tough to single out players, but skipper Conor Clifford, defender Jeffrey Bruma and Josh McEachran (tipped for the top in last season's Annual), were amazing over the two legs. Well done, lads!

The young Blues dominated the first leg but it took a curling Jeffrey Bruma free kick to earn a 1-1 draw at Villa.

Midfielder Josh McEachran had Villa's players falling all over the place with his clever touches.

"We had personal goals at the beginning of the season and I said mine was to lift the Youth Cup as captain, and I have done it now. It hasn't sunk in yet, it is brilliant"
– Conor Clifford

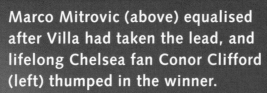

Marco Mitrovic (above) equalised after Villa had taken the lead, and lifelong Chelsea fan Conor Clifford (left) thumped in the winner.

With around 12,000 at the Bridge for the second leg the players enjoyed the acclaim as they lifted the trophy.

Even first team skipper JT got in on the act, congratulating the youngsters in the dressing room afterwards.

The pace and power of Turkish winger Gokhan Tore was important over the whole campaign.

HAVE I GOT BLUES FOR YOU...

An off-the-wall Chelsea quiz. How much do you know about your fave club?

1 How was Harry Potter linked to Chelsea FC last season?
A. The club added a blue wizard kit to its official merchandise offerings.
B. Chelsea ran a special train for supporters going to Sunderland from platform 9 3/4 at King's Cross.
C. Hermione Grainger (Emma Watson) came to the Bridge to watch the Blues.

2 Which Chelsea season ticket-holder took over as chairman of Liverpool FC in April 2010?
A. TalkSPORT presenter Andy Jacobs.
B. Former MP David Mellor.
C. Former British Airways boss Martin Broughton.

3 Who designed the players' new official club suits in July 2010?
A. Dolce&Gabbana.
B. Ant & Dec.
C. Cameron & Clegg.

4 Who gave Chelsea supporter Richard Hills, director of the Ryder Cup in golf, an old Real Madrid shirt with 'Beckham' on the back?
A. Golfer Sergio Garcia.
B. New Real boss José Mourinho.
C. David Beckham himself.

In January 2009, which Chelsea player accidentally struck a pigeon with a prematch warm-up shot on goal?
A. Didier Drogba.
B. Michael Ballack.
C. Salomon Kalou.

5

6 Who was spotted at Stamford Bridge wearing a Chelsea hat and scarf as the Blues beat Arsenal in February 2010?
A. Arsène Wenger.
B. Matt Damon.
C. Homer Simpson.

What song by Bob Marley & The Wailers became a Chelsea terrace anthem during the 2009/10 season?
A. 'Three Little Birds'.
B. 'Buffalo Soldier'.
C. 'Waiting In Vain'.

7

Answers page 61.

8 A Chelsea fan became a TV star by doing what on camera behind the manager's dugout during a game in November 2009?
A. Making 'bunny ears' behind Sir Alex Ferguson.
B. Brushing his teeth.
C. Offering Carlo Ancelotti a bite of his pie.

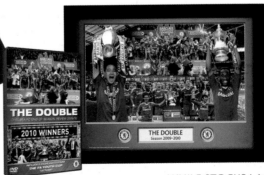

WE

"It is very good to have a celebration with our fans. There was a fantastic atmosphere and this improves the relationship between the fans and the team. In the future it will be important to have this good relationship" – Carlo Ancelotti

Chelsea supporters were fantastic as usual.

At the 'Double' victory parade the next day Carlo and JT couldn't stop singing to fans.

Didier produced an incredible bullet-powered free kick to win the FA Cup!

WEMBLEY!

Chelsea won the FA Cup for the sixth time in our history in May. Incredibly, it was our eighth appearance at the national stadium since it reopened in 2007.

Petr brilliantly saved a penalty from Pompey forward Boateng.

The boys lifted the trophy!

CHELSEA AT THE NEW WEMBLEY

19 May 2007	Man Utd FA Cup final	Won 1-0
5 Aug 2007	Man Utd Community Shield	Draw 1-1 (Lost on pens)
24 Feb 2008	Tottenham Carling Cup final	Lost 1-2
18 Apr 2009	Arsenal FA Cup semi-final	Won 2-1
30 May 2009	Everton FA Cup final	Won 2-1
9 Aug 2009	Man Utd Community Shield	Draw 2-2 (Won on pens)
10 Apr 2010	Aston Villa FA Cup semi-final	Won 3-0
15 May 2010	Portsmouth FA Cup final	Won 1-0

ROYAL BLUES
Chelsea's 2010 Award Winners

Once again this year the Chelsea supporters, players and staff voted for their best performers of the season. There were some tough choices to be made. Do you agree with the winners?

PLAYER OF THE YEAR

Golden Boot-winner Didier Drogba took this title for the first time in his six seasons here and demanded his teammates join him on stage.

"Wow! This is the happiest I have ever been and I want this moment to continue for years and years"
– Didier Drogba

GOAL OF THE SEASON

Ashley Cole picked up this award for his skilful solo effort against Sunderland.

"It was a great ball from JT. The guy dived in when probably he shouldn't have done. As I took the touch I did a 'Cruyff' [turn] and luckily the keeper went down and I chipped it over him"
– Ashley Cole

PLAYERS' PLAYER OF THE SEASON

Florent Malouda was voted the best by his fellow players following a fantastic campaign for the Blues.

"It has been one of my best seasons and I would like to thank my teammates. They are the best jury"
– Florent Malouda

YOUNG PLAYER OF THE SEASON

The whole under-18 squad won this for their efforts in winning the FA Youth Cup.

SPECIAL RECOGNITION AWARD

This special presentation was made to goalkeeping legend Peter Bonetti, who played 729 times for the Blues.

A SEASON BEHIND THE SCENES

It's not all about winning and silverware. (Okay, it is mostly.) But loads goes on at Chelsea every season that you will not have noticed. 2009/10 was no different.

POT THAT

The annual Cobham pool competition gives staff such as Gary the chef a chance to serve up a beating to the players. But when you're drawn against JT you are in a stew – he's brilliant.

SHOOT!

The players often have to help promote competitions such as the FA Cup. Salo was asked to pose for photos at Cobham before the Wembley semi-final against Aston Villa.

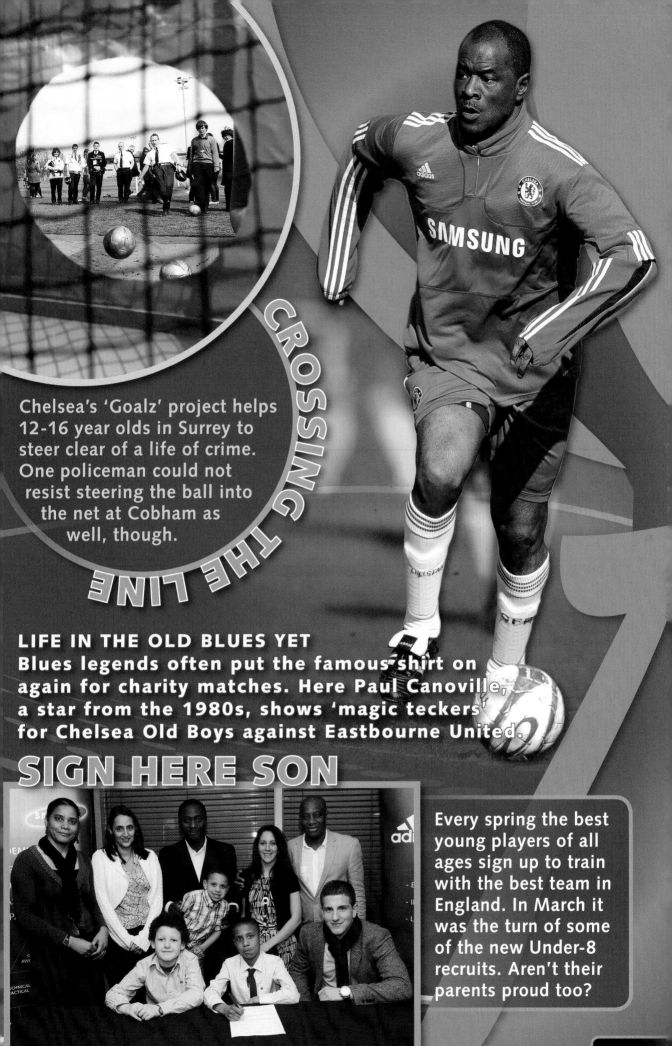

CROSSING THE LINE

Chelsea's 'Goalz' project helps 12-16 year olds in Surrey to steer clear of a life of crime. One policeman could not resist steering the ball into the net at Cobham as well, though.

LIFE IN THE OLD BLUES YET
Blues legends often put the famous shirt on again for charity matches. Here Paul Canoville, a star from the 1980s, shows 'magic teckers' for Chelsea Old Boys against Eastbourne United.

SIGN HERE SON

Every spring the best young players of all ages sign up to train with the best team in England. In March it was the turn of some of the new Under-8 recruits. Aren't their parents proud too?

A SEASON BEHIND THE SCENES

OH COME ALL YE FAITHFUL

Each year True Blue junior members can apply to have their name drawn out for an invite to the big Bridge Kids Christmas party at Stamford Bridge. It is a fantastic afternoon, attended by lots of players. Last year super Michael Essien joined in the fun.

PLAY TIME

While the older brothers and sisters are with mum and dad watching the football, younger members of the family can enjoy great facilities in the matchday crèche at Stamford Bridge. It was the first in the Premier League and is still the best run.

PLANE SPEAKING

Chelsea TV's Gigi Salmon will go everywhere to bring you the inside story on the Blues. In December she interviewed John Terry on a jet plane to Zurich before the FIFA World Player of the Year awards. Brilliant JT was named in the 'FIFA/FIFPRO World XI.'

CHAMPION STAFF

The people who work so hard behind the scenes for Chelsea wasted no time in meeting the latest arrival at Cobham in May – the Premier League trophy.

CHELSEA FOOTBALL CLUB

GREAVESIE FACT BOX
Born: 20 Feb 1940 in East Ham
Seasons at Chelsea: 1957-61
Chelsea appearances: 157
Chelsea goals: 124

JIMMY GREAVES
CHELSEA LEGEND!

On the day in October 1955 that manager Ted Drake saw his Chelsea side score five goals and still finish on the losing side at home, he received a phone call from the Blues' famous youth scout, Jimmy Thompson, a man who in his career unearthed more talent than even Simon Cowell.

'Never mind the game today,' said Jimmy, 'I've just found a boy who is going to be one of the best ever.'

He was talking about a lad from the East End of London, James Peter Greaves, and was delighted to tell Drake that the younger Jimmy had signed up at 16 to play for Chelsea's Junior team.

In 1956-7 Greavesie totalled an incredible 114 for the youth side in all competitions. It was no surprise when he was promoted to make his senior debut aged 17 against Spurs at White Hart Lane – and brilliantly scored the equaliser.

While Jimmy's greatest strength was his amazing goalscoring with either foot, he was also a lovely player to watch as he weaved through opposition defences with the minimum of effort.

Fans were very upset and angry to see such a favourite leave and carried him off the field after he scored all four goals in a 4-3 win over Nottingham Forest at the Bridge in 1961.

Fans felt even worse when Jimmy's stay in Italy went wrong. He returned to England and joined Spurs – not Chelsea!

Jimmy always speaks very fondly of his Chelsea days, and is still rated by many to be the greatest player who ever graced the Stamford Bridge turf.

Not bad for a kid signed from youth football for nothing!

"August 26 1957: Tottenham Hotspur 1, Chelsea 1. Ted Drake has made a rare discovery in this young Londoner who, with all the assurance of a veteran, slipped into the tempo of a battle waged to the last gasp before 52,580 roaring fans and scored Chelsea's equalising goal."

Soon the whole nation was paying attention and Jimmy made his England debut – and scored – against Peru in 1959, aged 19.

The young East-Ender enjoyed four brilliant seasons at Stamford Bridge, scoring 22 in his first campaign, 37 in the next, then 30, and finally 43 in 1960/1.

Jimmy piled up five goals in a game three times, and four goals on three occasions. Overall he managed an extraordinary 13 hat-tricks. While at Chelsea he became the youngest player to net 100 league goals, aged 20 years and 290 days – that is still a record to this day.

But in those days there was a limit to how much a footballer could be paid in England. That was not the case in Italy, and in 1960 it was announced that Jimmy would be moving to AC Milan for a huge transfer fee Chelsea could not turn down.

Jimmy's last match at Chelsea was against Nottingham Forest 50 years ago in April 1961.

QUIZ ANSWERS

Page 28 : Spot the Ball

A = 2
B = 5

Page 42 : Spot the Difference

Page 43 : Wordsearch

```
R D C F G M P M G D W I L K I N S C
K D L A S H E L L I T O J K R D A Y
R R L C L M C C R E A D I E L M H T
L F N S Z D N H X V T N W E P B L R
N N H C Z R E B K K G O I B T I C E
P O C O N T Z R L Z L F E T T M V H
M T N L L V B R H F R L N T Q I F C
W H R A X L H O H E L Q O W N L H O
L G D R F Y H C T T A L W W Q L I D
M I R I N N N R D F E D Z R K A D N
F N T M I A O C B C K M L H R I D L
M K T R L P R E N T N B T L M V I M
X L U B K H C A K N I T I D T C N D
M O B M O N R N N A W L X R H V R N
M Y K D W L M Q Y H R T L R R M M K
Z L D N C N O T X E S D F U X E L F
Z L R P Z H N N Y X Q R T B G M L N
E W M P R Y L Y I R E I N A R R R L
```

A : Ted Drake

Page 46 : Have I got Blues for you

1. C
2. C
3. A
4. A
5. B – the pigeon was unharmed (see www.youtube.com/watch?v=ktBWPOn1vkk)
6. B
7. A
8. B

WHERE ON EARTH IS STAMFORD?